Essays Irish and American

Essays
Irish and American

By
JOHN BUTLER YEATS

With an Appreciation by A E

Essay Index Reprint Series

 BOOKS FOR LIBRARIES PRESS
FREEPORT, NEW YORK

First Published **1919**
Reprinted 1969

'Homo sum; humani nihil a me alienum puto."

STANDARD BOOK NUMBER:
8369-1165-2

LIBRARY OF CONGRESS CATALOG CARD NUMBER:
70-88040

PRINTED IN THE UNITED STATES OF AMERICA

Contents

	Page
An Appreciation	5
Recollections of Samuel Butler	9
Back to the Home	23
Why the Englishman is Happy	37
Synge and the Irish	51
The Modern Woman	63
Watts and the Method of Art	75

AN APPRECIATION

E admire some because of their accomplishment, others because of what they are. I admire Mr. John Yeats as an artist as much as any, but I feel that nature's best gift to him was a humanity which delights in the humanity of others. Few artists I think found it more easy to be interested in the people they met or painted. All his portraits, whether of men or women, seem touched with affection. Rarely has he poŭrtrayed any, young or old, where something like a soul does not look at us through the eyes. I have liked people after seeing Mr. Yeats' portraits of them, and I am sure I would not have liked them so much if I had not first looked at them with his vision. In his delightful letters, of which extracts have been already published, and in his essays he lets us unconsciously into the secret of his meditation about his sitters. He is always discriminating between themselves and their ideas, searching for some lovable natural life. He complains in one of his essays that the

American women whom he admires cannot be easily natural. They want so much to be the ideal daughter or the ideal wife or the ideal friend that poor ordinary human nature is not good enough for them. He perhaps never heard of Laotze— how few people know of that fount of wisdom— but Mr. Yeats, who is, I fancy, unhappy in the society of metaphysicians, economists or theorists, would, I believe, have loved the Chinese sage who made a religion with this law, "Be ye natural." All the other religions draw us away from hearth and home and love and dominate us by an overlaw, but Laotze alone among religious teachers heaves a sigh when he hears of someone setting out to reform the world because he knows there will be no end to it. When Laotze says in his ideal state people would be contented in themselves, think their poor clothes beautiful and their plain food sweet, I think of Mr. Yeats and his fear that the reformer will improve the Irish peasant off the face of the earth. He delights in him as he is. Why should anybody want to alter what is already natural, wild and eloquent? To be primitive is to be unspoiled. Mr. Yeats seems to be seeking everywhere in art and letters for the contours and emotions which are the natural mould of face or mind. Mr. Orpen can astonish us with technical accomplishment and Mr. John with masterly drawing, but if we look at the face of a woman painted by Mr. Yeats we will be attracted, not by the transient interest of novelty in treatment, but because of some ancient and sweet tradition of womanhood in the face, the eyes, the lips. We find the eyes so kind that it is so we imagine mothers or wives from the beginning of time have looked upon their children or have bewitched men to build about them the shelter of home and civilisation. Mr. Yeats in his art had this intimacy with the heart's desire, which is not external beauty, as those who have degenerated art into the pourtrayal of prettiness suppose, but beauty of spirit. Those who knew Mr. Yeats will remember that enchanting flow of conversation which lightened the burden of sitting; and nature was wise in uniting the gift of conversation with the gift of portrait painting, because the artist was so happy in his art and so reluctant to finish his work; without that grace of speech few sitters could have endured to the end with an artist always following up some new light of the soul, obliterating what already seemed beautiful to substitute some other expression which seemed more natural or characteristic. To those who knew Mr. Yeats these essays will recall that conversation with which we did not always agree but which always excited us and started us thinking on our own account. The reader will find here thoughts which are profound, said so simply that their wisdom might be overlooked, and also much delightful folly uttered with such vivacity and gaiety that it seems to have the glow of truth. Perhaps these fantasies and freaks of judgment are as good as if they were true. One of the most delightful inventions of nature is the kitten chasing its own tail, and this and many other inventions of nature seem to indicate that a beautiful folly is one of the many aspects of wisdom. What is it but mere delight in life for its own sake, in invention for its own sake, or, as Mr. Yeats puts it elsewhere, a disinterested love of mischief for its own dear sake. How dear that is to us Irish who have often had nothing but love of mischief to console us when all the substantial virtues and prizes of life had been amassed by our neighbours. How witty Mr. Yeats is those who read these essays will discover. "When a belief rests on nothing you cannot knock away its foundations," he says, perhaps half slyly thinking how secure were some of his own best sayings from attack. I refuse to argue over or criticise the philosophy of the man who wrote that, for I do not know how to get at him. I am content to enjoy, as I am sure his friends will, and new friends also who will be made by a reading of this book, and who will be grateful to Mrs. Bellinger of New York, who cut out and preserved from various papers these essays as they appeared; for the writer, unlike the kitten, had no interest in chasing his own tail, and had forgotten what he had written or where it h l appeared. Gathered in one book these essays reflect a light upon each other and re-create for us a personality which has deserted Dublin, but which none who knew would wish to forget.

A. E.

RECOLLECTIONS OF SAMUEL BUTLER

KNEW Butler. In the year 1867-68 I was a pupil at Heatherleigh's Art School, Newman Street, London, and Butler was there also. It is not true that Butler had talent. To be a painter after the manner of John Bellini was for years the passion of his life. It was vain; he had no talent. At the time I knew him he was beginning to see this and it was pathetic! We tried to comfort him and would have cheered him with false hopes. All the intellect in the world won't make a painter if it is not the right kind of intellect.

A Scotch friend of mine and his, whom Butler loved because of his knowledge of music, would sometimes say, "Yes, Mr. Butler, you are a dominie"—and he would chuckle slowly in his Scotch manner. Like a dominie he kept us all in order. We called each other briefly by our surnames without the prefix of the Mr. — Butler was always *Mr.* Butler. Once a daring citizen of London ventured, "Have you been to the Alhambra, Butler?" He pronounced it "Al'ambra"—that gave Butler his opportunity. The Englishman in possession of all his aitches can always hold the many in check because of their deficiency in aitches. "Is there an aitch in the word?" said Butler. Never again did my poor friend venture, or for that matter any of us.

The Irishman likes his equal and is, as every one admits, the best of comrades; the German likes his superior; but the Englishman likes to be with his inferior and is not comfortable in any other relation. He is sent to the public school and the university by his anxious parents and guardians that he may acquire the superior manner. There are two sneers in England, the cockney variety which no one respects, and the university and public school sneer which compels respect, even among foreigners. It impressed Goethe. The footman puts it on but overdoes it, so that at a glance we know it to be counterfeit. Butler was the politest, the most ceremonious of men, but the sneer was there and all the more palpable because so carefully veiled.

We were art students and tried to be Bohemian, or would have done so had not Butler been one of us. There was a student whom he much liked; one day he took him in hand and in his most paternal manner admonished him that he must not use the word "chap." Butler was an Englishman through and through and an Englishman of "class." The Englishman of class will part with his faith, with his wife and children, with his money, even, or his reputation and be cheerful about it, but closer than his skin sticks to him his class conceit; and in his accent, his voice, his gestures, his phrases he carefully preserves all its insignia. Possessed of these he knows he may go anywhere and associate with anyone; it is a passport entitling him to a nobleman's freedom. Every Englishman, gentle or simple, either by force or by patient groping will try for a sheltered spot where he may have his own thoughts and his own ways hampered by none. But the Englishman of class is freest of all; a policeman, even he, will hesitate to interfere with you if he knows that you are a gentleman.

In his "Way of All Flesh," Butler describes English home life and he enables us to see that affection and sympathy do not form part of it. Butler, the product of that life, sets little importance on either affection or sympathy; and yet there never was a kinder man. Good nature was fundamental in his character and was, I think, the source of most of his writings and opinions. The English going about life in an intensely selfish way and doing this on principle are obliged to have strict laws strictly enforced; yet outside these laws they claim and allow the utmost license of action and thought. It is their distinction among nations that they love personal liberty so much,—that is for themselves, for they are quite ready to enslave other people. With this love for personal freedom has grown up, side by side with it and as part and parcel of it, an immense appreciation of human nature itself. Against this appreciation Puritanism has vainly and indeed dolorously struggled. Butler's good nature was due to his liking for human nature itself; hence his zeal against all the conventions and illusions and veiling " respectabilities " that would snatch from human nature its proper food.

The continental nations may hate human nature and produce their Goyas, but such art among Englishmen excites only a lazy contempt. Notwithstanding their passion for law and rule, a necessary thing among people so selfishly bent on their own gains, the Englishman does not actually hate his neighbour, even though he keeps aloof from him. He has indeed a genial relish for the selfishness in his neighbour which is so strong in himself. Edmund Burke has some such sentence as " the *good nature* and integrity of this ancient people." The Dutch, being a freedom-loving people, have a similar good nature. Rembrandt and Shakespeare get artistic pleasure out of the ugly but with laughter, not as in Goya with a grin of hatred. Indeed, looking at some of Goya's work, one is forced to believe that he hated even the people who looked at his pictures and wished through them to insult and offend all his friends,—a kind of disorderly impulse which in him and others prompts to the disgusting and obscene in art. Butler's emancipated intellect had won for his soul and senses a freedom which he wished to share with others; he had as it were acquired a freedom to be on good terms with himself. To be sure, a Scotchman is on good terms with himself when he is conceited. Butler wanted people to be on good terms with their senses and appetites and everything else that goes into our make-up as men, to all of which Scotch conceit is the enemy. For this he was always fighting, and he began to fight at Heatherleigh's Art School. He found us, as he thought, enslaved by this or that convention or illusion and by his mockeries and his wit worked for our liberation.

He always occupied one place in the school chosen so that he could be as close as possible to the model and might paint with small brushes his kind of John Bellini art. There he would stand very intent and mostly quite silent, intent also on our casual conversation, watchful for the moment when he could make some sally of wit that would crush his victim. He had thick eyebrows and grey eyes, —or were they light hazel? These eyes would sometimes look tired as he plied his hopeless task of learning how to paint. But the discovery of any mental slavery or insincerity among our band of students would bring a dangerous light into them, and he would say things that perhaps hurt very much men who were absolutely sincere, however mistaken. Then Butler, who respected, as he often told me, every kind of sincerity, would humble himself and make apologies that were not always accepted, and in the grey eyes, like a little fire on a cold hearth, I would see a melting kindness that it must have been hard to resist. The virtuous are not always the generous, neither are they always as wise as Solomon.

At that time I was a very busy student working from morning to night, otherwise I should have tried to see more of Butler. There is nothing so winning as a look of helpful kindness in a mocking face. Besides, he was a good deal my senior and seniority is attractive to ingenuous youth; and I was then ingenuous. I sometimes think I have lost all my opportunities; the chance of knowing Butler well was one of these. Slowly I have come to feel that affection for human nature which is at the root of all poetry and art, whether the poet be pessimist or optimist. Had I stayed much with Butler I should have learned my lesson almost at once. Matthew Arnold's " sweetness and light " was not much to his taste, and he cared nothing for the high ethics of Wordsworth. An affectionate mother, such as we have among the peasants of Ireland, where mother-love is a passion, does not want her children to be good half as much as she wants them to be happy. It was so Butler regarded poor, struggling and deceived human nature. *There* was the source of his " good nature " and of his influence. In this he was pre-eminently English of the English, and in this there was nothing of the system maker or the philanthropist. Nor was he a philosopher or anything else except a mere man touching and handling the concrete matters of everyday life. With tenderness of humour and a most real poetry he touched, healingly, all the sores of ailing humanity.

Butler liked women but disapproved of marriage. He liked women because, as I heard him say, they are so good natured. They would laugh with him but never at him. Then they are obedient and teachable and the dominie within him liked pupils. His attitude towards them was a smiling indulgence. The charming women of those backward days were still in the Middle Ages, apologetic, almost penitential, as if they asked pardon for being so beautiful or so merry and engaging, and did not a bit mind if Butler regarded them as inferior, especially as towards them he was always kindly and fatherly and innocent. It is quite easy to see why Butler disliked marriage; it would have curtailed his freedom to follow out all his queer vagaries of Butlerian thought and inclination. This consideration does not affect the ordinary Englishman of coarser grain, tenacious of his ancient right to do what he likes with his own, his own being his wife and children and servants and " all that he possesses." The ordinary Englishman lives alone in his English home, lord and master of it, with his wife second in command. Butler, of course, could not so live; therefore to keep his liberty he dismissed forever the thought of a married home. Had he married I have no doubt he would have chosen a helpmate not likely to dispute his supremacy. I knew Miss Savage, the model for his good woman in " The Way of All Flesh." She was a student at the art school and not very young, and she was lame; life had disciplined her. She was fair, with a roundish face and light blue eyes that were very sensitive and full of light; a small head, her features charmingly mobile and harmonious. She radiated goodness and sense. She kept herself very much to herself, yet all liked her, even though we never spoke to her. Butler soon discovered that she laughed easily; but as usual he was cautious. One day he consulted me as to whether he could with safety ask her a schoolboy riddle he had picked up somewhere, a schoolboy riddle in that, though quite innocent, it was not altogether nice. I don't remember how I advised, only that they became fast friends.

Though he avoided marriage, his flesh was weak. " I have a little needle-woman, a good little thing. I have given her a sewing machine. I go to see

RECOLLECTIONS OF BUTLER

her." As he made his confession he retired backwards, bowing his head several times as in mockery of himself and acknowledgment of a sad necessity from which even he was not exempt. For it was given to him also to tread "The Way of All Flesh." It was always part of his philosophy that he should confess his sins, besides being a necessity to his social nature and one of his most engaging qualities.

Though he professed to despise Greek plays he was a good classical scholar. Outside the classics he had read nothing except Shakespeare and "The Origin of Species" and the Bible. For him "The Origin of Species" was the book of books. If he took a fancy to a student he would watch him for a few days and then approach him with cautious ceremony—he was always ceremonious—and ask him if he had read *the book* and perhaps offer to lend it to him. I am proud to remember that he lent it to me. "The Origin of Species" had, as he told me, completely destroyed his belief in a personal God; so occasionally instead of the usual question he would ask the student if he believed in God. In this he did not confine himself to students. There was a nude model named Moseley who often sat to us at Heatherleigh's. He liked this model, in whom he found a whimsical uprightness that appealed to his sense of things. Once in the deep silence of the class I heard him asking, "Moseley, do you believe in God?" Without altering a muscle or a change of expression, Moseley replied, "No, sir, don't believe in old Bogey." The form of the answer was unexpected; its cheerful cockney impudence was beyond even Butler's reach of courage. He retired in confusion, and we laughed. We liked a laugh at Butler's expense. Besides, in those days most of us were orthodox; in fact had never given a thought to the question of Deity. But that fear kept them quiet, there were some valiant spirits who would have cried out against him, since then as well as now, in America as well as in England, an orthodox inertia was characteristic of artists. They do not go to church, they never give a thought to religion, but ,they are profoundly orthodox in a deep, untroubled somnolency. I remember that one man, a very successful student, did engage in controversy and was highly sentimental in a dandified, affected way. Butler's reply was one word repeated several times—"Pooh!" that ended it. I have no doubt that that gentleman still retains his orthodoxy. When a belief rests on nothing you cannot knock away its foundations.

Butler's father was a wealthy dean of the Church of England, and, I fancy, pompous and authoritative. He told me that his father never became excited unless the dinner was late. When he broke away from orthodoxy and announced his intention of becoming an artist instead of a clergyman, his family refused him all assistance. Nor is it true that his father helped him in his New Zealand venture. He himself told me that he managed to borrow from friends £10,000, and that he was more proud of that than of anything else in his life. He stayed in New Zealand four years, after which a lucky turn on the market enabled him to return to England and repay the money, while keeping enough to support himself in his pursuit of art. He liked to tell of his New Zealand life and of his hatred of sheep. They were always getting lost, so that he said the word "sheep" would be found engraved on his heart. He did not know one of his horses from another or from anybody else's horse, and said he was like the Lord, whose delight is not in the strength of a horse.

Sam Butler's desire for truth and his stripping away from life and belief all the veils of illusion was the characteristic of a man truly poetic. He and his pupil, G. B. Shaw, by their passion for sincerity, help the imaginative life. When Michael Angelo maintained that only the Italians understood art, Vittoria Colonna pointed out that the German pictures touched the feelings. "Yes," he replied, "because of the weakness of our sensibilities." Poetry and the imaginative life can only flourish where truth is of supreme moment; an education which contents itself with half-knowledge and half-thought will inevitably produce a crowd of sentimentalists and false poets and rhetoricians. The great artist and the great poet have rigorous minds. Michael Angelo said of those German pictures that they were only fit for " women, ecclesiastics and people of quality." After all a poet must believe, and without rigorous thinking there is no sense of belief.

To know things thoroughly, or not at all,—this was the habit of Butler's mind, derived from his classical education, in which the whole stress is on the minutiæ of scholarship. For instance, he told me that he never studied music till he was twenty-one years of age, after which he gave to it every moment he could spare. Yet he only cared for Händel, content that all the rest should be to him an unknown world. What he could not study thoroughly he would not study at all. In his eyes superficial knowledge was superficial ignorance and the mental habits engendered by it disastrous. Among painters he valued chiefly those who, like John Bellini, are thorough to minuteness. Though he professed to despise style he was a precisian in words. At a restaurant which he and I frequented for our midday meal he met a man who said he never " used " hasty pudding. This application of the verb " use " was to him a source of endless amusement. I have heard him tell the story many times.

I think he read Shakespeare continually. I know he read no other poetry, although he did glance once a little wistfully at Whitman,—" the catalogue man," he called him. All the same he was a genuine Englishman and brooded in the imaginative mood of a self-centred solitude which could not be shared with anyone, as the sympathetic Frenchman lives in the imaginative mood of an expansive existence which he would share with everyone.

I remember the last time I saw Butler. I was sitting at breakfast, alone, in a lodging in an out of the way part of London, having come from Ireland the night before after an absence of seven or eight years. I saw him passing and in glad surprise at once raised the window, meaning to hail him. But I reflected sadly and changed my mind, closing the window and returning to my breakfast, as I thought: " God forbid that I should intrude myself uninvited on any Englishman."

BACK TO THE HOME

EVERYWHERE or almost everywhere among English-speaking peoples the monarchical principle is under notice to quit. In the school it is the boy and not the master who rules; even in the courts the judges interpreting the law go cautiously, in fear of public disfavour; finally, change has reached the home and the family, which were wont to be a dual monarchy —the mother ruling within the house and the father his own world outside. Just as business is a matter of committees and syndicates and corporations— the individual man a mere wheel or pulley in some immense machine which is controlled by a cold-blooded arithmetician—so, inside the home, the mother is superseded by an expert, some specialist in up-to-date science or quackery who occupies her place and asks to sit where she sat. Can we wonder that she sometimes leaves vacant her chair and goes in pursuit of distraction?

It is a curious change and means much; for one thing, the world has lost its two most picturesque figures—the master of the house and its mistress. When hospitality was hospitality, it meant that you were admitted for a brief while to bask in the smiles of two gracious sovereigns—the lord and the lady of the house that entertained you—their good-will, radiating forth to warm you, the real attraction, to which the wine and the food and the guests were only secondary, so much heart on their side creating a heart within your own narrow ribs. Now all is changed, and the entertainment is more important than the entertainers. We come to be pleased, we no longer come to please; the old delicious autocracy with its smiling court of sympathetic and affectionate guests has tumbled into the dust, the feelings of host and hostess, the home cookery and the old-fashioned house with its gathered associations are nothing to us; we demand to dine where the food and drink are up to date, so we dine at a restaurant, where are noise, distraction and confusion. I myself would sooner dine in a good man's kitchen. Personal rule is at an end. The host used authoritatively to lead the talking and the hostess controlled it, for, though too busy to talk, she was never too busy to listen, and the guests took care that the conversation flowed in her direction and sought her approval. In my youth, after the dinner-things were removed, we sat around an ancient mahogany table, on which there was not, as in later times, any garish white cloth. It would have been gloomy but for the many-coloured reflections cast into its polished depths from wine-filled glasses and decanters and from the faces and dresses of the guests. Overhead were candelabra, the sole light in the room; outside the circle of diners such deep shadows that the faces looked like portraits by Rembrandt; and when, at the proper moment, the hostess and her ladies swept out of the room, leaving us to our men-talk, how lean would fall the entertainment! And it was our hostess we missed, so much divinity did hedge her.

The monarchical principle is extinct in the home, it is likewise extinct in the schools. I was educated at a school where the master ruled by terror. He was a Scotchman and knew no other method, and we were not in the least bit democratic. But if we trembled before him we did not fear one another. There were between fifty and sixty of us, a curious collection of diversities; not a boy in the place who had not something marked in him, either by his own strength or because of his home individuality. It was a time when parents had little money and travelling expenses were heavy, so that holidays were scanty and far apart. For instance, we never went home at Christmas. The cheap railway had not yet everywhere supplanted the mail coach. Yet we lived haunted by the thought of our homes,

—it possessed us, it obsessed us, it was our food and drink with which we fed our imaginations and spiritually nourished ourselves. We would talk incessantly to one another of our homes; and friendships, our only solace in that abode of sternness, were made up of similarities of taste and experience in the matter of homes. The methods of education were, if you like, brutal; but the brutality made our homes all the dearer. We leaned heavily on the thought of our homes; while in our happiness, as in our misery, we possessed a faculty of concentration unknown to boys educated in the latitudinarian methods of the modern schools. Whether it was our first Latin author, Cornelius Nepos, or our Latin exercises, or the horrible Latin grammar of that period, or the big Latin dictionary or Greek lexicon —implements of education whose repulsiveness was supposed to add to their efficiency—or our letters from home, or our long talks of home and yearnings for home—no matter what the subject, we brought to it an intensity that would have been foreign to the careless boys of this effeminate age. I remember a boy under twelve who talked to me in whispers of his father and mother not being friendly, and of his mother preferring to him his younger brother. There was another boy whose trouble was that there was so little money at home. There was yet another very little boy, who would take me aside and read long letters from a beautiful sister married

BACK TO THE HOME 27

to a military officer in India. Depend upon it, there is nothing that concentrates the mind like having for schoolmaster a conscientious Scotchman teaching Greek and Latin in the old clumsy methods.

A young boy is mostly regarded as something quite outside the pale of sympathy and understanding. Only his mother can endure him, and she because, as many think, love has made her blind. Yet in himself he is of all beings the most ingenuously and ingeniously human, and a veritable fountain of imaginative desire, who, if he do but retain his spontaneity, may become a Charles Lamb or a Coleridge or a Shelley; or, if he be built on the grand scale, a Dante or a Michael Angelo. The mission of the modern school is for the boys themselves to take in hand this little boy and, by force of their own rude animalism and with joyous pressure, strip him of everything exceptional and compel him to take on another likeness. I remember an English lady telling me that she had been to visit a great public school to see her son, a little boy. She told me that at a distance she could not distinguish him from any other boy; and she smiled helplessly as she added that it was the ambition of every little boy in that famous school to be exactly like the other little boys. And yet we wonder that the world no longer produces distinguished individualities. This mother knew that her boy would come back to her the average boy, to grow into the average man, like his father, like his uncle, like everybody else. A friend of mine, a most interesting man, very happy in his hobbies and in his dreams and visions and beliefs, a poet though without learning, and without the sweet accomplishment of verse, lamented that he had not been kept longer at school, where, as he said, he might have had all the " nonsense knocked out of him." The poor fellow does not know how happy and interesting he is; he only knows that his wife and all his friends find him different from other people and on this account disapprove of him. Yet there was an old French artist in 1830 who advised his friends to cultivate their faults carefully.

The old methods were brutal and made the boys brutal, yet they, at any rate, did not break down and insidiously destroy singularity of character as is being done every day by the democratic methods of modern schools. A celebrated master of Eton in the eighteenth century said, " My business is to teach Greek, not morality." In that robust century people did not take much thought about one another. You might be unhappy and all astray, but they let you alone; provided you did your Greek right, your morals were your own affair. Chatham may have left Eton a " cowed " boy, as he implied he did, yet he brought with him an individuality of a quality so angular and so challenging that it is impossible to believe it could have survived had it been ground between the upper and nether millstones of modern school-boy life. These schools, both in America and in England, with their great prestige and with the boys in full control, have become so powerful in moulding character that it is no longer accurate to say " the boy is father of the man," but rather, " the school-boy is father of the man." In Ireland things are different. The old brutal methods being discarded, the boys do not fear the master, neither do they fear each other, and the explanation is that the Irishman, man and boy, gentle and simple, is much more of an aristocrat than a democrat. He belongs to his home and to his family; he has the passion for home and family, he passes through school or college without really belonging to either of them.

For that reason the home among the Irish remains stronger than any school or college, exactly the reverse of what has happened in England and may happen in America. When I say an Irishman, gentle or simple, is an aristocrat, I do not mean that he is a person of class or wants to be one, or that he bears the slightest resemblance to the modern English nobleman, but I do mean that he likes to think that he is a person of distinction, and that he differs from all other men, and values himself accordingly. Nature herself would, if we did not thwart her, evolve each man on a different plan; as she makes every leaf and every twig and every tree in the forest different from all its fellows. She has an Irish delight in diversity, and smiles to see her sturdy children each fighting for its own hand.

The typical Irish family is poor, ambitious, and intellectual; and all have the national habit, once indigenous in "Merry England," of much conversation. In modern England they like a dull man and so they like a dull boy. We like bright men and bright boys. When there is a dull boy we send him to England and put him into business where he may sink or swim; but a bright boy is a different story. Quickly he becomes the family confidant, learning all about the family necessities; with so much frank conversation it cannot be otherwise. He knows every detail in the school bills and what it will cost to put him through the university, and how that cost can be reduced by winning scholarships and prizes. As he grows older he watches, like an expert, the younger brothers coming on, and is eager to advise in his young wisdom as to their prospects. He studies constantly, perhaps overworks himself while his mother and sisters keep watch; and yet he is too serious, and they on their side are too anxious for compliments. It is indeed characteristic of the Irish mother that, unlike the flattering mothers of England, she loves too anxiously to admire her children; with her intimate knowledge there goes a cautious judgment. The family habit of conversation into which he enters with the arrogance of his tender years gives him the chance of vitalizing his newly acquired knowledge. Father, mother, brothers and sisters are all on his mind; and the family fortunes are a responsibility. He is not dull-witted, as are those who go into business to exercise the will in plodding along some prescribed path; on the contrary, his intellect is in constant exercise. He is full of intellectual curiosity, so much conversation keeping it alive, and therein is unlike the English or the American boy. Indeed, he experiences a constant temptation to spend in varied reading the time that should be given to restricted study. He is at once sceptical and credulous, but, provided his opinions are expressed gaily and frankly, no one minds. With us intellect takes the place which in the English home is occupied by the business faculty. We love the valour of the free intellect; so that, the more audacious his opinion, the higher rise the family hopes. He and all his family approve of amusement—to do so is an Irish tradition unbroken from the days before St. Patrick; but they have none. They are too poor and too busy; or rather they have a great deal, but it is found in boyish friendships and in the bonds of the strongest family affection, inevitable because they are Irish and because they have hopes that make them dependent upon one another. The long family talks over the fire, the long talks between clever boys on country walks—these are not the least exciting amusements—even though they bear no resemblance to what is called " sport."

These are the gifts of the Irish home; among the poor, affection infinite as the sea, which, because of an idleness which is not their fault, has had full scope to grow into an intensity of longing that makes it sometimes hungry as the sea; among the better-off, ambition also and a free intellect; and in everybody an ancient philosophy of human nature which warms rather than chills human relations.

The English boy has an entirely different history. He enters some famous historical school, anxious, like his parents and all his aunts and cousins, that he be stamped and sealed with its approval. His desire is to be an Eton, Harrow, or Rugby boy, after which he will become an Oxford or Cambridge man, marked in his accent, clothes, and manner with the sign-manual of his university. For the Irish boy this is as impossible as it is repugnant. His home is stronger than his school and his college. In the great English schools the boys manage one another; a system of rules and of etiquette has democratically grown up which all must obey; this kind of docility is English and not Irish. Our boys cannot thus surrender themselves, for behind the Irish boy is the drama of a full home life. There is no such drama in English home life—it is prosperous, uneventful, and lies icily cold in the lap of law. The Irish home, in which so much happens, awaits its novelist; but, alas! English readers won't read novels about Ireland, and Irish readers are too few to make their custom worth anybody's attention. All we know is that the Irishman is, boy and man, a detached personality. He is often the gayest and most sociable of beings, and a true comrade, and he may be able to adapt himself to every situation, yet he remains apart; even with his friends he is inscrutable, he cannot be read. And this to my mind is right, for no one should be able to read another's secret, except the mother who bore him, and sometimes a sweetheart. The ordinary well-to-do Englishman has no secrets, for you can read them all in his bank-book, in his Catechism, in the rules of his club and the laws of his country. He is an admirable citizen on whom you can calculate as on a railway time-table. The English mother when she parts from her boy at the school doors may sigh to think that she has lost her boy, yet be proud to think that he will return remodelled into the smart Eton or Harrow boy. The Irish mother has no such hopes and no such fears; her boy will come back what he was when he left her side, and though he go to India, and rule provinces, with many well-trained public-school Englishmen working under him, he will still remain the passionate Irish boy of her heart's desire.

The great factor in the Irish education is not the

school, but the Irish home, unique in its combination of small means, intellect, and ambition with conversation. Without this conversation the home would not be Irish. From every manor-house and cabin ascends the incense of pleasant talk; it is that in which we most excel. With us all journeys end in talkers' meeting; "we are the greatest talkers since the Greeks," said Oscar Wilde. When any Irish reform is proposed—and they are innumerable —I always ask, how will it affect our conversation? France has her art and literature, England her House of Lords, and America her vast initiative; we have our conversation. We watch impatiently for the meals, because we are hungry and thirsty for conversation; not for argument's sake or to improve ourselves, but because we spontaneously like one another. We like human voices and faces and the smiles and gestures and all the little drama of household colloquy, varying every moment from serious to gay, with skill, with finesse; we like human nature for its own sake, and we like it vocal —that is why we talk; we even like our enemies, on the Irish principle that it is " better to be quarrelling than to be lonesome." Arthur Symons, staying in a pilot's cottage on the west of Ireland, said to my daughter : " I don't believe these people ever go to bed." No, they have so much to say to one another.

" England," said Bernard Shaw, " cannot do

without its Irish and Scots to-day because it cannot do without at least a little sanity." Both these nations are conversational.

The home must play its part vigorously if the race is to be saved for affection and happiness, and if we would bring back the conditions from which spring art and poetry.

WHY THE ENGLISHMAN IS HAPPY

An Irishman's Notes on the Saxon Temperament

N the long quest for self-knowledge and self-fulfilment there are two types of men and two methods. There are some who would have the individual man care only for himself morning, noon, and night, for his spirit, his mind, his body, his temporal and eternal welfare. There are others who would say he should forget himself and lose himself in great ideas, great causes, great enthusiasms, in passionate love or humanitarianism, or even in the anger of battle. Of these two methods the second is found in France while the first is the Englishman's creed.

The English are a fortunate people, or seemed so in the happy past, their primal good fortune being that they lived and grew up on an island surrounded by stormy seas and fenced in by high cliffs. Their second good fortune sprang out of the first; they never submitted themselves to a strong central government. Of all people in the known world, they were the least governed; of all men the Englishman was the freest, little more being required of him than that he should live on good terms with his neighbours. Doubtless one of these neighbours was the brutal Norman noble who regarded him as an inferior being of an inferior race, and as a landlord oppressed him. Outside this relation of landlord and tenant, and of superior and inferior, he lived a free man among his fellows without, indeed, the dignity and honour of being a soldier, but also without his constant subjection and unrelaxing discipline. He was a boor, but his thoughts were his own; and his language, being different from that of his oppressor, afforded him an additional protection. He lived in his own world—he lived apart among his own race and kindred.

The other nations on the continent of Europe, notably France, lay open to one another's ravages; and for that reason had always to remain under arms, every man a soldier, martial law superseding all other laws. However England might war with other nations, however she might despoil them, pursuit and revenge were impossible; behind her cliffs she was safe. No matter how great the cloud of hatred or what it threatened, she lived in security and laughed at her enemies. The peasant returned in peace to his village and his plough, the merchant to his shop, and the noble to his castle; while crimes

WHY THE ENGLISHMAN IS HAPPY 39

that could not be punished left no visitings of remorse. The English grew in liberty and in the arts of peace while other nations grew in the arts of war and lost their liberty. The English poor man was never taught his military dignity, but he was taught his social inferiority; yet, while he bowed down, as he still does, before his social superior, his thoughts remained free; the better part of liberty remained to him. Froissart was astonished at the squalor in which the English peasant lived; yet, had he looked a little closer, he would have seen that under the smouldering ashes on his hearth a fire was burning that had long been extinct in his own country.

The French government was a military despotism, and since tyranny begets tyranny and seeks to extend itself, it speedily drew to itself the forces of religion, art and education, and allied them in one vast conspiracy against the forces of freedom; so that from the first the people were trained in submission to power, authority and tradition. It was an eager and spontaneous submission, the soldier proud to follow his captain, the student eager to listen to his teacher, and the Catholic anxious to obey the command of his priest. The people were accomplices in their own enthralment; the more so since there was this discretion reserved in the exercise of dominion : all were free to think out and draw their own conclusions, provided that the State, the Church, and the academies furnished the premises. Deductive logic was free; inductive logic, the higher order, the kings, soldiers, magistrates and statesmen kept in their own hands. As time advanced the French became a nation of teachers and orators as well as soldiers, while the creative impulse was everywhere arrested and hampered. Welded together and bound and clamped into a nation by their military and ecclesiastical organizations, the French rapidly acquired the instinct of solidarity; and the individual dwindled until he became a mere unit of the state. This feeling of solidarity combined with the free exercise of deductive logic, resulting in a fertility of beautiful ideas—beautiful as rainbows on a stormy sky—and the missionary habit. Of all men the Frenchman is the most picturesque and the most attractive, as he is also the most eloquent and the most persuasive. In literature, in life, in everything, the French genius is social and sympathetic and propagandist.

The Englishman is the contrary of all this. He has a passion for liberty and cares little for equality, fraternity, or any of the ideals which are the glory of the French intellect. He is, indeed, so entirely without the faculty of ideas that even his feeling for liberty has never become an idea or a doctrine; he has no intellectual cognizance of it; it is merely his habit. A something which from long use has grown into him and become part almost of his physiology, it is in his blood and in his bones and remains by him always, keeping vigilant watch and ward. But it is for himself alone; it is not for universal application; it is not his philosophy. So that when he robs another nation, as in the case of India or Ireland, and, in order to facilitate the theft, first takes away that nation's liberty, his conscience does not smite him, for by liberty he always means English liberty, which includes the privilege of robbing any nation that is weak enough to stand it. To me a Frenchman is always like a student; either as he is when he works diligently at his studies or as he is when he plays truant, breaks away from discipline, and defies his teachers. An Englishman, on the other hand, is a person untutored, who has never been either to school or to college; he has neither the attractiveness of the diligent student nor the excesses of the rebel student. He is still almost what he was when he came first from his Maker's hands.

Besides his exemption from military organization and a central government, there is yet another fact to be noted in the Englishman's history. A peaceful immigration into his country has been as difficult as a warlike invasion. In other countries, when the population was reduced by plague and pestilence, the void was quickly filled up by an inrush of hungry foreigners; in England this was impossible. There a sudden fall in population meant a sudden rise in the abundance of food, because there was no one to come from outside to take the food out of men's mouths. The population of mediæval England remained always small. The Englishman's native joviality and ease of heart were his song of triumph over a condition in which, if he managed to survive, he lived easily and fed well and clothed himself warmly. If other people died, so much the worse for them and the better for him. To this day the Englishman takes extraordinary care of his health. The French and Irish contempt for death is to him a continual and a shocking surprise. He never needed to work hard; he faced no great struggles; he merely took care of his health.

In those far-off days of ease, little work, and much mortality the Englishman acquired all his habits, all his positive and negative qualities, together with that fear of death which we know oppressed Dr. Johnson; and though the last hundred years have much blunted his characteristics, the pattern still remains. He is still given to much self-contemplation in its various forms of self-complacency, self-examination, self-condemnation, and self-exultation. He talks continually of himself; deprived of that subject and of what is akin to it, he is a silent man. Not to be the subject of conversation, neither to be praised nor abused, is to him a disconcerting experience. He is not vain; it is merely that his occupation is gone. The

Americans are too busy with their own growing fortunes to remember his existence, and for that reason he is, here in New York, either so gentle and sad or so peppery and quarrelsome as to be quite unrecognizable. He is no longer himself. In his own country he is an unwearied egotist. When pleased it is with himself, when displeased it is still with himself. With his neighbours he is often sulky; yet his worst quarrels are with himself, and therefore the hardest to reconcile. His variations are variations not of idea, but of mood. The French live in a ferment of opinion; it is their atmosphere—man contending against man with noise, vociferation, oratory, and much action and movement. Among the English there is always the silence of inward communing, the stillness of a people overweighted with meditation. In France new schools of art and movements in literature are the triumphs or—it may be—the eccentricities and freaks of the logical process. In England such movements mean the welcome or unwelcome emergence into light of a new species. French impressionism was ushered into the world with loud argument. Turner's art was something inscrutable and mysterious, the expression of a temperament that did not argue and looked for no converts. Under any strong excitement the Englishman withdraws into himself as into the security of his own home. The Frenchman, on the contrary, gets away from himself into the world of friends and ideas and starts a propaganda to embrace the world. He seeks to impress; his literature and art are full of dramatic surprises, while English art and literature have always avoided startling effects; and, if they impress, do so accidentally, as a tall mountain might the people who lived in the valley. They continually spring forth from the mysterious depths of personality, and, concerning themselves only with moods of feeling, rely for expression on rhythm and music. A personality cannot explain itself or account for itself; it can only cure its ache and soothe its irritability by the music—the long-drawn-out or fantastic music of artistic creation. French art and literature concern themselves with ideas, and their effort is to make these brilliant, orderly and specious, using the emphasis and animation and sonorousness of art rather that its deeper music. So that in France they watch for a distinguished intellect, while in England we look for an individuality that is at once powerful, strange, and intimate, its expression intelligible only to those who have explored the farthest recesses of consciousness. In France we find a garden, in England a wilderness. Yet, do not forget, the gardener will often visit the wilderness in search for new plants and shrubs. The inductive mind sows that which the deductive mind plants out and waters.

The egotist is popularly supposed to be a wearisome chatterbox incessantly talking about himself; and such men do abound in England. An egotist is any man who habitually and instinctively makes himself, his likings and dislikings, the sole test of truth; and it is only when there is some streak of folly or childishness that he becomes the garrulous chatterbox. Of these men some are delightful humorists, as was Charles Lamb, or undelightful, as was his boisterous brother John. Among them are, in fact, all sorts, including all the bores, cranks and faddists, with the innumerable company of monologists; including also the great pioneers and forerunners of thought in poetry and art: the Shakespeares, Turners, Hogarths, and Constables.

Socially, the egotist, where there is not some great compensating charm, is a failure; he does not amalgamate; he is ever an alien in the company, a difficult person. You don't know whether to make much of him or drop him altogether. At a dinner-party the Englishman is apt to be that sad mistake, a guest who has to be apologized for. Lovers are always poor company except with each other. This is proverbial, and the Englishman is always in love—that is, with himself. The sociable man, the welcome guest, is in love with other people. As it is in the lighter matters of social intercourse, so it is in graver matters. Gladstone, who, as a

Scotchman in England, was an acute critic, once wrote that the Englishman needed a great deal of discipline; and this is true. A community whose members are not spontaneously amenable to one another's feelings must have definite rules laid down and enforced by definite penalties. On the other hand, the Frenchman, with his social impulses and social training, knows "how to behave." He does not need to get rules by heart, for he has intuition; and where he has not this inner light he turns naturally to reason, the great sociable spirit, the friendly arbiter, the wise judge before whom all men are equal. The English egotist has not this social impulse; neither does he willingly appeal to reason. Latterly he has become saturated with class feeling, which is neither sociable nor reasonable; but his original instinct, to which he constantly returns, is to regard himself as neither a superior nor an inferior, but different; a humorist who cannot be classed and to whom no general rules can apply; and such a man will not readily appeal to a tribunal before which all men are equal.

The Frenchman is a gentleman; he has the finer instinct, the finer training, and the finer intelligence; wanting these, the Englishman has to be taught by the cumbrous methods of reward and punishment; he learns under the whip and becomes more like a well-trained animal than a reasonable human being.

WHY THE ENGLISHMAN IS HAPPY

Yet—such is the blessedness of mere habit—even he ends by doing quite cheerfully what he learned most unwillingly. Legality, hard-and-fast rules that must not be broken and that are interpreted in the narrowest spirit, depressing enough in all conscience although they be, are to him an enjoyment and a matter of incessant thought; since if they circumscribe, they also define and secure the spaces of personal liberty. They are his substitute for ideas, and, if they excite no enthusiasm and are some of them admittedly bad, all the same, he makes it his glad duty to obey them. Outside these laws he is intractable and inclined to be surly, quarrels with his neighbours, and is as jealous and suspicious of his rights as a dog with a bone. Yet the Englishman is not unhappy. He has the happiness of a perpetual self-complacency. Indeed, your self-absorbed egotist will sometimes extract enjoyment of a kind out of the consciousness that he is a wet blanket and a perpetual embarrassment and kill-joy; it does not quicken the pulses, but it flatters his sense of power, and, strange as it may seem, his sense of hatred. At any rate, I have met such men both in England and elsewhere. And yet there is another side to the picture; for this self-contained egotist, when trained in a good school and taught the amenities of good behaviour, and when he has received the discipline which Gladstone said he so much needed, utters the best kind of talk, since it flows not out of the logic which divides, but out of the inner personality which makes the whole world kin. There is in his conversation almost always a flavour of the intimate and the confidential. He listens well, too, and never contradicts or seeks to convince. Indeed, it disappoints him to find one opinion where he thought there had been two. Cultivated Englishmen talking together are like men sitting in the woods through a long summer's night and listening during the intervals of silence to the noise made by a near-by stream or of a wind among the branches or to the singing of a nightingale. So always should mortals talk: clamorous and confident argument are the resource of the intellectual half-breed.

Out of his habit of mind the egotist gains two valuable qualities. First of all he learns how to manage himself. This, of course, is not the same as the high and difficult art of self-mastery, yet it counts for much that a man should know how to get the best and leave out the worst from his life, even though that life be in its essential mean and meagre or vicious and self-indulgent. Self-management, smooth and adroit, is eminently the Englishman's accomplishment. The other quality is still more important; the egotist makes the best of all husbands if regard be had to the ordinary woman's needs; for what are these if they are not all summed

WHY THE ENGLISHMAN IS HAPPY 49

up in the one word—companionship? Now a wife cannot find a sufficing companionship in her husband's business concerns. Here she is beaten by the confidential clerk. There is, however, one kind of friendship, one kind of companionship, which she alone can supply in the required abundance; it is when the husband talks of himself. Here is the chamber into which the wife enters willingly when everybody else keeps away: the husband's talk of his pains and aches and tribulations. There is the pain in his knee or his elbow, or the never-to-be-sufficiently-indicated pain in his head or his back, or his cough, and how it differs from every previous cough in his experience, or bears a dangerous resemblance to some other body's cough, together with the innumerable aches of his wounded and exaggerated self-love. All this wearisome detail about what is mostly nothing at all and which everybody else flees from, the " pleasing wife " listens to with an attentive and intelligent and credulous ear. It is her duty, or so she thinks it, and the greater the intelligence the greater the credulity. There are happy wives married to husbands whom it would bore to talk about themselves, but the happiest woman, in whom content ripens to its fullest, is the egotist's wife. Like a bee in a flower, she hides herself almost out of sight in wifely devotion. He finds happiness in living in and for himself, she in living out of herself and in him. Both are pleased. This is English conjugal life as I have observed it; and here in perfection we have side by side our two methods of human growth.

SYNGE AND THE IRISH.

THE acrimonious dispute carried on in the newspapers over John M. Synge and his plays is the eternal dispute between the man of prose and the man of imagination. Synge's plays, his prefaces to his plays, and his book on the Aran Islands, like his conversation, describe a little community rich in natural poetry, in fancy, in wild humour, and in wild philosophy; as wild flowers among rocks, these qualities spring out of their lives of incessant danger and incessant leisure; there are also bitter herbs. When I used to listen to Synge's conversation, so rare and sudden, as now when I read or listen to what he has written, I can say to myself, "Here among these peasants is the one spot in the British Islands, the one spot among English-speaking people, where Shakespeare would have found himself a happy guest."

The people in Mr. Shaw's plays would not have bored him, only because nothing human would have ever bored Shakespeare; but they would not have inspired him. And though in their company he might have stayed for a time and been perhaps as witty as Oscar Wilde or Shaw, the lyrical Shakespeare, the poetical and creating Shakespeare, would soon have tired of their arid gaieties, and have gone to sit with the courteous peasants round their turf fires, that he might listen to their words, musical sentences, musical names, folk tales, and tales of apparitions, embodying images and thoughts and theories of life and a whole variegated world of lovely or bitter and sometimes savage emotion out of which to construct poetical drama—a very different thing from the drama of wit or satire or sensationalism whose inspiration is prose.

It was Synge's luck that he found this people before the modern reformer had improved them off the face of the earth. Each of us has his destiny, and this was his. Every event in his life and every chance encounter did but help to push him along till he found his real self by living among them in the intimacy of their family life and in the closer intimacy that came from speaking with them a language into which they put their inmost feelings and longings, using English for what was merely external. It was his destiny to know these people and reveal them, and then die; and to be denounced as an obscene and indecent writer and artist by a set of people who will not listen and therefore cannot know, and whose service to Ireland consists in striving to shout down every distinguished Irishman.

SYNGE AND THE IRISH

Synge's people are primitive in the sense that they are unspoiled. A lady of fashion among the Chinese would regard the foot of a European woman as primitive; we think it is unspoiled. Synge's offence consists in showing that these people have never been moulded into the pattern that finds favour with the convent parlour and in the fashionable drawing-room. New York is proud of its progress and makes pretensions to high culture; and yet New York might do worse than turn aside and learn of these humble people. A young girl told a friend of mine that what she and her companions always look forward to in Ireland are the long winter evenings around the kitchen fire when the neighbours come in to talk. I fancy all New York is in constant conspiracy to cut as short as possible its dull winter evenings.

In Ireland we are still medieval, and think that how to live is more important than how to get a living. When I was a young man if I announced that I intended next morning at break of day to start on some enterprise of amusement, or it might be of high duty, the whole family would get up to see me off; but if it were on some matter of mere commercial gain, I would breakfast in the care of the servants. It was thus through the whole of Irish life. If Curran, for instance, fought a duel in Phœnix Park at some unearthly hour, five hundred sleepy Dublin citizens would rouse themselves out of their beds and be there to see the fight, to witness the courage of the combatants and enjoy the wit of Curran, that never failed when danger threatened —and in those days and in that country people shot to kill. We Irish are still what we've always been, a people of leisure; like people sitting at a play, we watch the game of life, we enjoy our neighbours, whether we love or hate them.

Because of this enjoyment of the spectacle of life, we have produced the ablest dramatists of latter-day England: Farquhar, Goldsmith, Sheridan, Oscar Wilde, G. B. Shaw, and finally John Synge. And of these, Synge, though he died so young, is the greatest. He stands apart from them all, because he portrays peasant poetry and passion, and a humour which cuts deep into the mystery and terror of life. In the other dramatists we have abundance of wit and liveliness, great powers of enjoyment, and a commendable contempt for the prudential virtues; but there is also a denial of spirituality and but a modicum of poetry; the deeper feelings are never sounded, while their pathos is only a dainty pity, not the genuine article: not one of them could have written "Riders to the Sea." Behind the Irish humour and pity are will and intellect, as in Swift. In the drawing-room plays of Synge's predecessors there is merely the sensitive nature, so easily chilled by what is not nice, becoming, and charming. Those who object to Synge's plays are suffering from the delicate stomach of people who have lived effeminate lives. Dr. Swift would have come to Synge's plays and applauded them.

A good many years ago cultivated people and others began to take an interest in the Irish peasant; it added something to the gaiety of London and Dublin drawing-rooms. But socialism and communism, the labour party and anarchy, had not then been invented to teach people the seriousness of starving poverty. So Carleton and other writers set to work to exploit the Irish peasant and make him into something " fit for a lady's chamber." Hence has arisen the foolish tradition that the Irish are all gentleness and innocence, and, though wildly amusing, still within the bounds of good taste; hence also came the comic Irishman, a buffoon without seriousness who lived by making laughter for his patrons.

Synge's plays exist to prove the contrary of all this. And yet there is some truth in the picture. The Irish character has a side which is turned toward spirituality and poetry, a musical instrument exquisitely attuned to the beauties of nature and life. Among this fighting race, square-chinned and with short features, is scattered another type, with long, oval faces and soft eyes, born to all hoping gentleness and affection, with imagination fed on the mysteries of life and death and religion.

This type Stella might have discovered had she not been too English; Swift could not, because probably he frightened it away. Yet Dr. Goldsmith was as true an Irishman as Dr. Swift. How vividly Synge knew this side of the Irish mind is shown in his book on the Aran Islands. The other side is in his plays.

"A picture," said Blake, "should be like a lawyer presenting a writ." Synge presents us with such a picture. Let us be patient; people brought up on the literature of good taste cannot be expected all at once to enjoy the literature of power.

"I can look at a knot in a piece of wood until I am frightened by it," so spake William Blake. This is the creative imagination, and it is that of folklore and of the Aran Islands. These people know no distinction between natural and supernatural; they believe everything to be carried on by miracle; and the civilized man who does not know that behind all science and reason and all moral systems there is a something transcending all knowledge and which is a continued miracle of love and beauty is not only incapable of culture, he is incapable of desiring it. To him the Bible is as inscrutable as Shelley. These peasants are not as well educated as, say, Mr. Rockefeller, yet they have this feeling, this feeling which is the religion of children and poets, and which is not subject for reason at all—even though it be the source of our whole intellectual life.

False education is like the pressure which the Chinese mother applies to the feet of her infant. True education liberates. The industrial movement would turn these peasants into smug artisans, without a thought that consoles or a hope that elevates, greedy, envious, and covetous, seeking only the triumphs of selfishness. And yet man is naturally a singing bird; sometimes he is singing in a cage of childish and brutish ignorance; and sometimes, though the cage be roomy and handsome, he does not sing at all, has not the heart to do so. True education would liberate him so that he could sing in the open sky of knowledge and power and desire.

Synge says of these people that they have " some of the emotions thought peculiar to people who have lived with the arts." He also speaks of " the singularly spiritual expression which is so marked " on the faces of some of these women. And again he says that " they are a people whose lives have the strange quality that is found in the oldest legend and poetry." A priest told me that on his return from America the servant said she was glad to see him back, " for," said she, " while you were away there was a colour of loneliness in the air." In these people's words, as in their lives, is the colour of beauty, as the blue sky reflects itself in every little pool of water among the rocks.

As to Synge's great comedy, "The Playboy of the Western World," could Synge have chosen a better type for his hero than Christy Mahon? Despite certain newspaper critics who have written of the play, he is neither a weakling nor a fool, but a young poet in the supreme difficulty of getting born; only in this case the struggle is a little worse than usual. He has a drink-maddened father of great strength and most violent passions, whose cruelty, backed by his strength, has driven away all his family except this young boy. Of course, Christy has no education, and his circumstances are altogether so dreadful that to live at all he must live the life of the imagination, wandering on the hills poaching and snaring rabbits. Finally he strikes his father with a spade, and in his terror runs away from home. After travelling for many days he arrives in Mayo and finds himself a hero; not because he is a murderer, but because he is a good-looking fellow in distress, and, as the sequel proves, spirited withal and athletic. His talk about the murder is a sudden freak of self-advertisement; no one so cunning as your young poet! Besides, he liked to be frightening himself. No one really believes it, and the Widow Quinn is scornfully sceptical; and when, later on, as they think, he actually murders his father, every one turns against him—his sweetheart, though it breaks her heart, joining actively in handing him over to justice.

SYNGE AND THE IRISH

In every well-constructed drama there is some central point of interest around which all the other incidents are grouped. The personality of the girl Pegeen, Christy's sweetheart, is here the central interest. She towers over every one, not only by her force, but by her maidenly purity and Diana-like fierceness; nothing, neither the coarseness she herself utters in wild humour, nor what the others say or do, can soil her sunshine. And in the love-talk between the lovers, he is all imagination and poet's make-believe, and she all heart and passion and actuality, which is the peasant woman's good sense! It is among peasants of the west of Ireland that the poetical dramatist must henceforth find his opportunity. Young gentlemen and young ladies in America have doctrinaire minds; they have grown up attending classes and listening to lectures in the atmosphere of a specious self-improvement, and know nothing of the surroundings amid which this peasant girl grew up straight and tall as a young tree. Some day people will recognize in this play Synge's tribute to the Irish peasant girl. "And to think it's me is talking sweetly, Christy Mahon, and I the fright of seven townlands for my biting tongue. Well, the heart's a wonder, and I'm thinking there won't be our like in Mayo for gallant lovers from this hour."

The peasants of the west of Ireland are like Christy Mahon; sorrow and danger and ignorance are their daily portion, yet like him they live the life of the imagination. Liberate them from what oppresses, but so that they may still live the life of the imagination.

Synge's history was peculiar. He took up music as his profession and studied it in Germany, Rome, and Paris; and having only a very small income, for economy's sake always lived with poor people. In Paris he stayed with a man cook and his wife, who was a *couturière*. He told me that they had but one sitting-room, in which the man did his cooking and the wife her sewing, with another sewing-woman who helped. When, as sometimes happened, a large order for hats came in, Synge, who by this time had given up music for philology, would drop his studies and apply himself also to hat-making, bending wires, etc. After a year or so he moved into a hotel, where he met my son, who urged him to leave Paris for the west of Ireland and apply himself to the study of Irish. Among these western peasants he thenceforth spent a great part of every winter, living as one of the family, they calling one another by their Christian names; and he told me that he would rather live among them than in the best hotel.

Synge was morally one of the most fastidious men I ever met, at once too sensitive and too proud and passionate for anything unworthy. He was a well-built, muscular man, with broad shoulders, carrying

SYNGE AND THE IRISH

his head finely. He had large, light-hazel eyes which looked straight at you. His conversation, like his book on the Aran Islands, had the charm of entire sincerity, a quality rare among men and artists, though it be the one without which nothing else matters. He neither deceived himself nor anybody else, and yet he had the enthusiasm of the poet. In this combination of enthusiasm and veracity he was like that other great Irishman, Michael Davitt. Like Davitt, also, he was without any desire to be pugnacious; resolute, yet essentially gentle, he was a man of peace.

THE MODERN WOMAN

Reflections on a New and Interesting Type

QUEEN ELIZABETH, we know, had many lovers, but was herself never in love; and so she was able to get the better of her cousin, Mary Queen of Scots, who, poor soul! allowed herself to be ensnared by the tender passion. Queen Elizabeth, on the historic page, is a monster. Yet what was singular in her is now quite general.

It has been America which has given the world this strange type; like everything else that happens in this country, she has sprung suddenly upon us, as if she had neither father nor mother nor any visible ancestry.

She may be in a minority, yet she is not difficult to discover, for she is most active, showing herself everywhere. Nor is it difficult to describe her, since she spends much of her time in describing herself. In the first place, like the orator, she is made rather than born; indeed, she is herself a good deal of an orator, always being ready to harangue her friends, explaining and enforcing her ideas. Self-improvement is her passion; improvement in what direction? you will ask. She herself does not know. Meantime she insists on absolute personal liberty—moral, physical, mental, and also political. That she may be free she places a ban on the senses and upon sex; either of these would put her back under subjugation. She announces herself to be eager for affection, but its object must be some person who is supernaturally perfect and complete; anything else would be illogical and unworthy and enslaving. And while her mother dreamed of a life of love and duty in a world where both are necessary because of its sorrowful imperfections, she will be satisfied with nothing less than a perfect love and a perfect affection. At the same time, while resolved on liberty she does not forget that she is born into a business community; therefore she has adopted the business man's creed—efficiency: "Whatsoever thou doest, do it with all thy might."

The young men know liberty to be a chimera—that vision has never flattered their eyes. Life to them means hard work and obedience and a constant struggle in circumstances where everything is compromise, and where even honesty is not always the best policy; and as to success and the making of money, even the greatest energy will not suffice if there be not good luck and the opportunity. Unlike the women, these young men have their dreams, for dreams are the solace of labour and abstinence: dreams, first of all, of success and fortune, of which they constantly speak; and then another dream not so easy to talk about: that each may marry some day the girl of his choice.

Here you have American life as it is among the young. The man under discipline and a dreamer; the woman a triumphant egotist, and without any dreams at all. And as to this liberty which she haughtily demands, what is it, among the girls, except the right to choose and dismiss her teachers, abandoning everything and everybody as soon as she ceases to feel interested? Never having been curbed, she has not learned to prefer another to herself. In vain nature cries out within her for the sweet burden of service and sacrifice; she is much too busy listening to her own voice, repeating its new catch words: "I will be myself, I belong to myself, I must lead my own life." Once she enters society and becomes a woman and meets men, she acquires a very definite purpose, and goes straight for it. Since she will not serve the men, let the men serve her. "The American woman," said a languidly insolent Englishman to me, "are interesting; the men are nonentities." In the Englishman's conception, the man who does not take the upper hand with his women is a poor creature.

The ladies in England do not like the modern American woman. Her success with their own menkind is bitter to bear; yet they envy her. For these men are serving woman as they never served before; and it is precisely because, like the Englishman, the modern woman is herself an egotist. Egoism the Englishman understands: it has always been his honoured creed and his practice; and here at last is a woman who, because of her frank selfishness, is perfectly intelligible; no longer the mystery she used to be, but simple like a child's puzzle. Her frantic, brand-new egoism is not quite the sober article he patronizes for himself, but it delights him nevertheless, because it is so like his own daily contest with antagonists whom he must overcome in business. And here is a beautiful enemy, whom he must both overcome and capture and carry away with him as a prize of war; to be the ornament of his house and a delight to the eyes, to be his courtier, his worshipper, his wife; and as to the extravagance of her egoism, he feels that as a man he can soon teach her a different lesson, so that she will settle back into tameness and play her woman's part, and be his English wife. And even if she does not, consider what an advantage it is to have within doors a wife who is perfectly intelligible, and with whom he knows what to do! Why, he can be as logical in his own home as in his place of business. The woman used to be the greatest mystery in the world—you might defy her, or be kind and yield to her, or crush her with your iron will; but you couldn't understand her. No man could read that riddle. The writers of comedy, the writers of tragedy, all tried their hands at it. Satirists and wits were never tired of the fascinating theme. Yet it was all guess-work. No one pretended to know, and the husbands least of all. Henry the Eighth, who cut off the heads of his wives, knew no more than last year's lover. Such used to be woman. Now she is as easy to read as an old almanac. Watch her as she paces Fifth Avenue, with her businesslike air. How bright her eyes, and yet hard as jewels! Her smile how thin-lipped! and her figure that of a young athlete. Her mode of dress and of personal array, how smart and efficient and almost military! She is the very embodiment of briskness, and of commanding decision. But all the lines of allurement are vanished, and she no longer undulates with slow grace. She is not feline, neither is she deerlike; and she no longer caresses, for her voice is as uncompromising as her style of dress. The ordinary man, unless he was a gentleman of the old school, or a high-placed nobleman, or an Irish peasant, has always despised the arts of pleasing, until some charming woman has taken him in hand; but the modern woman has ceased to instruct him, and has become his imitator, so that her manners are almost as intimidating as those of the successful business man. Where is that threefold charm of mystery, subtlety and concealment, under which womanhood was wont to veil its powers; and while so many bow down before the conquering woman, where are the poets? The astronomers, the mathematicians, the scientists, the men of business, the lawyers, especially the lawyers, *are* at her feet, but no music comes from the poet; and she—is she so happy?

Egoism is unhappiness for man and woman. Talleyrand called Napoleon "the unamusable." It used to be the man who was egotist and the woman who served, for she said: Our mission is to please. Hence her all-prevailing charm, and hence also her invincible happiness, for happiness is the denial of egoism. However it be at other times, the happy woman and the happy man are righteous—in man's sight and in God's.

Happiness is the secret known only to poets and to women; and it was the women who taught it to the poets. Mere man knows little about it; least of all the successful man, for risking everything he has mostly lost everything; under his prosperity there is generally distaste. And how sorrow and disaster can at times degrade a man we all know; he becomes gloomy, bitter, or drearily self-contained, or he drops into dissipation and becomes vulgar. The woman, on the other hand, finds in disaster her opportunity; and sorrow, which the woman's life seldom escapes, however it be with the men, only intensifies her womanhood, so that she anticipates a later wisdom, and luminously refuses to recognize any distinction except that between the happy and the unhappy. There are only two people who are perfectly content—a woman busy in her home and a poet among his rhymes. They have the secret; they share it between them; they break bread together, they are of the company, even though the poet knows nothing of domestic life nor the other of rhymes. The true, the natural woman is like a bird, she has wings. When she is a young girl she is like a bird just spreading her wings for flight; when she is a matured woman she is like a bird in full flight: desire gives her wings, and stirs within her the creative impulse; and nothing can stop her strong flight towards happiness. She has the creative gifts—wherever her eye lights, there is happiness—she gilds with " heavenly alchemy " whatever she touches.

The resolute, practical man puts away the thought of happiness, and for it substitutes pleasures, which are the gratification of the senses, and his unquenchable thirst for variety and movement. These gratifications he can resign with little effort —mere pleasure is ashes in the mouth, while the other he thinks would unnerve him; that is for poets, he will tell you. The woman does not believe in pleasures, she believes in happiness. A supreme belief in happiness is the woman's soul. It awakens in her the moment she is in love or has a child, and accompanies her everywhere. It explains, I think, the curious self-centredness of her mind, and that strange aloofness which seems to envelop her who has husband and children. In her presence we talk of this and that, and do this and that, and she watches us with eyes in which is the light of knowledge and foreknowledge.

The man is a worker and a fighter; with strenuous effort he pushes along the car of progress, and dies under its wheels; and we make lamentations. But these women should be carried to their graves with song of hope and wistful triumph; any other kind of music would be wounding to our recollections. A man talks mysticism and he argues; and I am bored. A woman looks and perhaps smiles, and almost as by the touching of hands communicates her own unfading hopes. She does not use words, and we do not oppose her with words.

Long ago people talked much of ladies' eyes, and ancient Homer, as we know, sang of the ox-eyed Juno and the azure-eyed Minerva. Now ladies' eyes are too bright and too exacting to be so eloquent, so persuading; and for all her dominating ways she is not the queen she was, nor for all her witchlike effectiveness is she so calmly beautiful.

THE MODERN WOMAN

By turning egotist she has dropped down to our level. She is one of us.

And yet the modern woman is right and has arrived in the nick of time; she is needed because the modern man is not always a gentleman. Some fifteen years ago I was witness to a strange scene on Kew Bridge, outside London, one Sunday morning. A line of five young ladies came riding by on cycles, wearing bloomers. This excited the loud derision of some loafers, some half-breeds, standing together on the side-path, and one of them said something, I did not know what, but the last of the girls heard it and understood. She stopped, and, carefully adjusting her machine so that it stood up against the curb of the side-path, walked back to the young man and asked him if he had used the offensive words; she then knocked him down, and he fell, probably not so much because of her strength as because of his own surprise. Sheepishly he got up, brushing his clothes, and his companions laughed as sheepishly, while she remounted and rode after her friends. Here was the modern woman but immature, effective on this occasion, yet much too crude for anything except a guerrilla war. In Belfast, famous for its bad manners, every one tries to be "boss" over some one else; yet if every one can't be "boss" in Belfast, there is no man even now who cannot find, both in Belfast and New York and everywhere else, a woman whom he may "boss." This is one of the solid comforts of the masculine existence; but young ladies teaching in the public schools are watching sympathetically the career of the modern woman.

It insults a woman nowadays to say that the woman's destiny is to be always dependent on some man; but we who say this know perfectly well that it is equally true to say of the man that it is his destiny to be dependent on some woman. These two must patch up their differences. Man must yield to woman equality and dignity; and she must take him back into favour. There is no such companionship as that between a man and a woman. She brings her wisdom, traditional with her sex, and derived from a long study of the question how to live, and he brings his energy, derived from his long study of how to make a living. When energy makes him say, Let us forget the present and think about the future, she will reply: Let us enjoy the present—am I not young? Is not the childhood of these children exquisite?

People forget or do not know that man's desire for liberty is not greater than his desire for restraint. By practising the art of happiness he gets both. The gratification of all the desires, tempered each by each, is happiness—hope restrained by memory and the lust of the flesh by affection and sympathy; herein is richest harmony and a servitude which is perfect freedom. Pleasure is the gratification of some one desire pushed to excess and followed by weariness and satiety; and while pleasure overwhelms intellect and silences it, happiness makes intellect supreme. Happiness enforces discipline spontaneously; pleasure relaxes it and brings on licence, which is the shadow of liberty and its final destruction.

It is character, they say, that saves the world. Does this mean the will that is strong to grasp and hold? If so, then I know of something infinitely greater: the full and varied knowledge that comes from the whole complex human personality—every instrument in the orchestra—being developed in our consciousness, so that no single desire is "refused a hearing," as in a good democracy where every citizen has his rights secured. Here we have the benign wisdom of Shakespeare and of good women, and its motive is the deliberate search for happiness; it kindles the heart and shines in the eyes of a beautiful woman when she goes about in her home and among her friends and neighbours—beautiful and a sceptre-bearing queen; because in a world where every one runs mad after this and that falsehood, she stands for the simple truth of human happiness and all its possibilities. Wisdom is better than force, and supersedes it.

WATTS AND THE METHOD OF ART.*

I HAVE often wished that some great painter had written his autobiography, beginning with his earliest childhood. Saints and sinners have left us their memoirs in more than sufficient detail; and we have also the autobiographies of many famous writers.

As yet we have not had the confessions of the Painter; for I am sure they would be called confessions, since it would have been with a sense of shame that these men, including the magnificent Michael Angelo himself, would have confessed their failures at school to learn as other boys learned, and receive, as other boys did, instruction from their teachers.

We are all familiar with instances of boys who, exceptionally quick and clever to ordinary observation, are almost unteachable at school. It would be

* A report of a lecture delivered in the spring of 1907 at the Hibernian Academy, Dublin.

thought cruel, as well as impossible, to attempt teaching grammar and arithmetic to a young musical genius in a concert-room where musicians were playing; yet this is precisely what is done every time we try to teach grammar and such things to a boy with the eyes of a painter. Time and experience have at last taught us to be respectful and tender with the musical mind; we accept, and we understand it; and the boy with the wonderful ear is caught up and carried away and instructed and fondled, and the world is made smooth for him. But how about the boy with the wonderful eye? And yet the musical boy is only tempted when music is actually being played, whereas this other is never free from solicitation, since to him there is always, except in the dark, colour and form and light and shade. He will know the shape and surface of every object in his schoolroom, and how light falls on desk and table; he will know among his school-fellows all the profiles and all the front faces, what colour the eyes are, and how they are shaped; every detail of form and colour will be familiar to him, since to watch these things and to draw from them a continuous, intellectual intoxication is the very purpose for which he has been created; for with him the eyes are the gates of wisdom; and with young children these eyes are so thronged by wisdom trying to get in that all their time is taken up in opening the gates to its inrush.

In this progress of the painter—in this preparation for what, if the conditions are favourable, ought to be the solemn business of painting or sculpture—there will be various stages. At first it will be all observation; after that will come a time in which the boy will make inferences; to him the face will be the index of the mind; and, looking round on master and boy, he will be a physiognomist who has never heard of Lavater, or a craniologist or phrenologist, until some happy moment when, having exhausted his interest in scientific inquiry, there will burst upon him the glorious world of intellectual desire.

A friend of mine—an old painter, who went to school in the North of Scotland—described to me his experience. The dominie had one morning been particularly drastic in his methods, and this led to great concentration of thought among the pupils, while at the same time it did not in the least alter the usual current of their ideas. My friend, for instance, busied himself as usual, observing form and colour, only with a keener zest and, as I have said, a more concentrated purpose. It was a spring morning, and, for the first time that year, a ray of sunshine came into the room, making a square of yellow light on the dusty floor at his feet. It was only at that particular period of the year such a thing was possible: later on there would be too many leaves on the trees, and in winter the sun was not in that quarter of the heavens. My friend was an unhappy and anxious schoolboy, but the events of that morning and the menaces of the dominie, combined with the sudden sunlight at his feet, made a new boy of him, and he looked at the square of brightness which stirred his heart. He received, as it were, his mystical message; and some time afterwards, leaving school, he became a landscape-painter.

With a man like Mr. Watts the world of desire would have burst differently. He was the greatest figure-painter England has ever produced. With the exception of Blake, who hardly counts, I may say he was the one painter who worked in the grand manner and on great subjects. Years ago, by a happy accident, I met him in my studio. I remember his handsome face and a certain air, as it seemed to me, of imperious detachment; in his voice also there was a touch of austerity. He looked at my pictures without a word, till I asked him for his opinion. It then came clear, frank, and to the point. I did not tell him what, nevertheless, was the fact—that, though I had never seen him before, I had been his diligent pupil for years, and that from him first I learned the true meaning of painting, and why I, or indeed anyone else, had been induced to take up the craft.

All his days Watts was a hermit and a recluse;

had he loved life and enjoyed it, he would have lived in it and painted it, as Hogarth lived and painted; yet he loved his fellow-man, and sought unweariedly whatever made for his happiness: indeed it might be said that he painted because he loved his fellow-man. With such a man the world of desire must have burst in some scene that excited his indignation or his pity, or his moral admiration and love, and from that moment he would become a dreamer who incessantly re-builds life, according to the dictates of a kindled imagination; for since the eye finds what it looks for, the world of desire becomes in the self-same moment the world of creation; the desiring eye is the creating eye: the world itself is neither beautiful nor ugly; it is a formless vast out of which we create, according to our desires, new worlds; the madman and the poet look out on the same scene, but where the one finds ugliness the other finds beauty; and the world Watts looked out on was the world of men when they suffer or when they strive together in serious purpose.

In speaking about Watts, I would begin with his portraits. As regards these, there is no controversy; some people harden their hearts against his pictures, but no one denies his portraits. Now it seems to me that the genius of portrait-painting is largely a genius for friendship; at any rate, I am quite sure that the best portraits will be painted where the relation of the sitter and the painter is one of friendship; and it considerably helps my argument to know that in Watts' case he mostly painted people whom he had himself invited to sit.

The technique of portrait-painting is mainly a technique of interpretation; to get the colour, to model the face adequately, this to the practised hand is comparatively easy; to so paint that people should, perforce, see the particular curve, the particular shadow, and the particular shape of brow or eye that interest the painter; here is the true difficulty, here the true enjoyment and exquisite triumph of the painter.

In his early portraits there is little attempt at this interpretation. There is, indeed, the charm of atmosphere never absent from Watts' work at any time, and there is a very obvious decorative purpose; but these early portraits do not grip the attention as the later portraits do, because the technique of interpretation is lacking.

I have heard people say they liked his male portraits better than his portraits of women, but I cannot share this preference; each in its degree is perfect. Watts will paint a young lady in fashionable evening attire—surely the most modern and up-to-date arrangement possible—and he will so paint her, so gild her with the heavenly alchemy of his art, that she shall appear like a Venetian beauty gazing at us from the page of history.

Indeed, over all his portraits, whether of men or women, he spreads a sort of dim religious light; so that while painted with Dutch realism, they yet seem to come to us out of the mists of memory and romance.

Before speaking of his pictures of imagination, I will discuss a little the whole purpose of art and artists.

The moralist says: I teach morality, without which society would not hold together.

The trader says: I teach trade, without which there would be no wealth, and life would not be worth living.

The religious teacher: I teach religion, without which people would forget that there was another world or a judgment to come.

And the scientist says: I teach truth, which is the basis of everything.

What can the artist say for himself in presence of this congress of teachers, before whom we stand silent with hats off in age-long reverence?

First, what is his record?

He works only to please himself, and regards it as the most egregious folly—indeed, a kind of wickedness—to try and please anybody else; he admires wrong as often as right; at one time he occupies himself with the things of the spirit, and again he turns just as eagerly to the things of sense; without conscience and without scruple he flatters in turn every passion and every instinct, good or bad; he will make the unhappy more unhappy, and the wicked he will make worse; he inculcates no lessons, and preaches no dogma; yet often the noble will become nobler for his companionship.

He is to be found in every community; among the sinners he is a sort of father confessor, whose absolution is light, so that you may confess all your sins to him, and you may still go on sinning; he will laugh at the faces of the good, finding them guilty of self-complacency, of formalism, of insincerity, of prudence, of cowardice, of half-heartedness; indeed he is often much more respectful to sinners than he is to good people of the earth; and withal is it not from the hands of the painter and the poet that, as in some royal caprice, the hero receives his crown?

This strange creature with the dubious record; what use is he in the scheme of things? He seems to stand outside the whole circle of the utilities.

Why there is morality, why there is commerce, and why there is science, and why there is religion; these questions are easy to answer. But why there are painters, and sculptors, and poets, and musicians, is another mystery; it is as if you asked me why there are billions of suns rolling through illimitable space.

Among these august teachers the mere artist stands like another Lucifer among the angels. And

WATTS AND THE METHOD OF ART 83

yet all these teachers, high and mighty though they be, pay to the artist continual court, and would fain make him one of themselves : would indeed rescue him as a very wanton from his bad surroundings, and persuade him to live with them always; and this partly because human nature is strong within them, and they love the craft we practise, and partly because they recognize that where men are gathered together the artist—that is, the poet, the painter, the musician, and the sculptor—wields, for good or evil, the mightiest power on earth. Where is the theologian that the poet does not help? Where is the moralist? At the present moment, here in this exhibition, it seems to me that, in their astute way, the theologian, the moralist, and even the metaphysician, all think that they have patched up an admirable working arrangement with one of the greatest of our artists.

The titles "Love and Death," "Time, Death, and Judgment," "The Temptation of Eve," "The Penitence of Eve," "The Contrition of Cain," etc., do perhaps explain the facts that in Scotland Presbyterian ministers crowded the Watts' Gallery; and also that here in Dublin, for the first time in the history of our animated city, a splendid collection of pictures has been shown, and the voice of detraction and malignant criticism remains silent.

Well! do these pictures teach anything? Has Mr. Watts been captured? Is he a theologian or a moralist, or a metaphysician? Or is he merely a highly-gifted man, working out his salvation by way of art?

Take his two pictures of Eve. In all this collection there are none more poetical.

In the first of these, "The Temptation," what have we? A woman in the fulness of her magnificent animalism, and we have this animalism in the moment of its highest provocation. She seems to curl herself and to quiver with delight as she listens to the whispers of the subtle serpent; how voluptuously she leans over to the tempter, her body elastic with health and vitality. It is womanhood; it is splendid animalism, as yet untouched by conscience or doubt, and unchilled by the thoughts of death; all about her summer flowers and rich perfumes. At her feet a leopard rolls, itself a faint echo or reverberation of her vast personality.

It is the merest sophistry to call this moral teaching; it celebrates the deliciousness of temptation as Pindar, the ancient poet, celebrates the wine-cup. In both these pictures Watts celebrates the beauty of the nude and the beauty of the flesh. Leighton would have painted Eve grand and statuesque—a figure out of the penumbra of that decorative world where nothing is quite real. But this woman, colossal and demi-god though she be, is as real as one of his portraits—that of J. S. Mill, for instance, or the Earl of Ripon. She is so real, that you feel almost that you could touch her golden flesh, and hear her cries and murmurs of delight; while the other Eve is so realistically painted that it might be said she weeps audibly.

Next take his picture of Paolo and Francesca. Of all pictures in this gallery it is the most complete, possibly because his friends liked it, and gave him the encouragement all artists need. It is at once beautifully imaginative and a piece of charming decoration. But these poor guilty lovers, these wrecks of humanity, these fragments of tenuity, afloat on the winds like dead leaves, like lightest gossamer, teach no moral lesson. This picture illustrates afresh the sad fate of true lovers, and makes their punishment tender and beautiful. I should like to have had John Knox's opinion of this picture. There was a certain grimness, a certain severity in the painter. A meeting between these two champions would have been interesting.

Yet we are so hemmed about with difficulty, and so bewildered by a multitude of counsellors, and have got so much into the pestilent habit of seeking guidance everywhere, that one must needs find a moral even in the bosom of a rose.

Therefore—although it be quite unnecessary to the true appreciation of art—I will, reluctantly as it were, entirely on my own responsibility, pluck some moral guidance from imaginative art.

If morality frames for our guidance rules of conduct which, if we do not obey, we are to be punished—if it bids us shun temptation and remove temptation from our path and from the paths of all the world—Art, on the contrary, seems to say, with all its strength and with all its voices: " Seek temptation; run to meet it; we are here to be tempted." Art does not say—" Be happy, or be miserable, or be wise, or be prudent "; but it says—" Live, have it out with fortune, don't spare yourself, be no laggard or coward, have no fear." And this also is part of the message: " Abide where Watts lived, and where the true artist always lived—on the high table-lands, in the unshaded sunshine of intellectual happiness—never descending into the valleys, where hang, mist-like, the languors and lethargies, the low miseries, sensualities, and adulteries which afflict human nature when it is defeated, discouraged, disintegrated."

At the end of this room there is a large picture enormously impressive—" Time, Death and Judgment." To be impressive is itself a great artistic merit; yet I do not think this a great picture; there is, indeed, a fine arrangement of colour, and mass, and line, yet behind it all there is no energy of conviction.

Time moves forward, a striding figure, carrying a scythe; beside him walks Death, his wife, a weary woman, tenderly gathering into her lap the flowers of life; above these two figures is Judgment. These figures are vague and conventional as regards any meaning or intention they might convey. If this picture has any meaning, it is as if Watts had said to himself : " I am a figure-painter and will, by my craft of figure-painting, translate into a picture the kind of pleasing terror which is excited by watching a fine sunset or listening to an oratorio." This is not art, as Michael Angelo gave it. Blake said a picture should be like a lawyer presenting a writ.

"Love and Death" seems much finer—it grips the attention at once. Before the other picture we stand idly pensive; but here we want to get at the root of the matter—to grope our way into the very heart of the picture. There is the naked figure of Love, wavering, falling backwards; and then Death, this huge bulk; draped, and hooded, and horrid. Is it man? Is it woman? and its face is hidden; and is this because it was in the thought of the painter that no one has ever seen the face of Death except the piteous dead, who carry their knowledge into the grave?

As regards a famous picture not in this collection —the picture called "Hope"—I would say that, pleasing though it be, it owes its success mainly to its faults; and that people like it because no one can say exactly what it means. A man who really lived by hope—a Krapotkin or a William Morris— would find its vagueness utterly displeasing.

England likes her artists to preserve a soft, indefinite touch, because in her world of action and practical effort ideas must not be pushed too far, and compromise rules. Art, on the contrary, does not like half thoughts—she will have a positive yea or nay. If thought is not pursued to its furthest bourne and limit, the picture lacks energy, and is without effect. In Art, as in everything else, energy is the true solvent.

In my mind, pictures of this kind are meant to hang in the rooms of the idle rich—because intended for people who wish, without effort, to indulge themselves—and see all things past, present, and to come, rosily and smilingly, however falsely. There are artists, poets, and painters—and in this case Watts is among them—who seem to keep in stock a sort of pharmacopœia of drugs and opiates and soothing mixtures to be served out as required. Michael Angelo owed his terribleness, his black melancholy, to the fact that in his pride he would not accept any soothing mixtures; he faced all the facts of life.

Now, let me say a word in reply to those who are so ready to point out defects in Watts' technique. To find fault is easy—is at all times easy. In this vivacious city it is a special accomplishment, where, indeed, everyone has learned logic, but no one has learned enthusiasm, and few care for the ideal or for poetry.

WATTS AND THE METHOD OF ART 89

In answer to these people I would enter a plea of confession and avoidance.

Granted all they say about these faults, I would ask, in all the roll of English painters, is there one who would have given us that magnificent Eve of the Temptation? How royally she leans forward as she stoops to her fate: what swing and what pose in her movement. In the strain, in the ecstacy of her sinning, every nerve and every muscle seems to tremble. Not Millais, nor Leighton, nor Alma Tadema—far more accomplished artists than Watts —could have done it; nor Reynolds, nor Gainsborough, nor Vandyke. None of these men had the technique to do what Watts has here done. Watts triumphs by his technique.

But it has not been always so in Watts' work. When not roused to great exertion by his theme, he fell away into carelessness and into haste. You see, this man who lived so long a life had such a teeming mind that his hands could not work fast enough.

And here let me allude for a moment to Watts the man. All accounts that have reached us represent him as singularly humble and modest. It was so with Michael Angelo, and it is so with all men who work among great ideas. When The Last Judgment was finished, and all Italy burst into praise, and princes, cardinals, and poets, vied with each other in presenting homage, Michael

Angelo waved them off with scorn. "If," he said, "I carried Paradise in my bosom, these words would be too much"; and he wrote in reply to one of them: "I am merely a poor man, working in the Art God has given me, and trying to lengthen out my life." When an artist or poet gives himself airs, puts on side, as we say, it is because, like Lord Byron, he is working away from great ideas, and because in all simplicity and good faith he finds nothing which asks his reverence, nothing greater than his own fortunes and his own sensations. Art for Art's sake is for those who hate life, as many poets do, or who hate ideas, as again many poets do. The great artist is also a man like unto ourselves, and great personality is the material out of which is woven all his Art.

Now, let me offer most respectfully a startling opinion. I think that as a religious painter Watts failed; and that he failed because he was bound to fail.

The spiritual world is as much with us as it was with the people of the fifteenth and sixteenth centuries; but we seek to explore its recesses, by tabulated observation, by sequences of thought, by scientific guesses, and carefully planned experiments: things not to be expressed in pictorial or plastic forms, even though Michael Angelo has said everything might be expressed as sculpture.

Is it that Nature never repeats herself? She has

produced her religious painter; his day is over; and Watts was trying to do what was impossible.

In those far-off days people believed—and actually, with the most vivid realisation, believed—at one and the same time in angels, archangels, and saints, and gods, and goddesses, and prophets, and sybils, and fiends of the under-world, and all the machinery of the supernatural, including angels, such as that which Watts has painted in the picture "Love and Life"; and the painter who painted those images worked under the exacting criticism of an alert and expectant people. Now, in place of these beautiful or terrible personages, we have substituted the forces of nature.

Examine his picture called "Love and Life." It is a vast subject. The whole mind of the civilized world is groping a way among its problems. But this picture is wholly inadequate. Life is represented as a feeble mendicant sort of creature, blindly stumbling up rocky stairs. This is a poor image of life. Milton would have scorned it. Watts should have remembered his own "Eve." And "Love" is represented as a strong angel. It is precisely because Love is not a strong angel that all the trouble is upon us. If his picture of "Hope" should be placed in a lady's boudoir, this picture should hang in the cabinets of those who think life is to be saved merely by the clasping of hands and turning eyes heavenward.

In "Eve's Repentance" there is a cold light bursting through the blue clouds, and shining over the back and shoulders. We have here the old Venetian harmony of blue and yellow and white; and because of it, in some subtle way, we have an enhanced sense of the warmth of the palpitating, naked flesh. But, bless you! this is not all. By this light breaking through the clouds, Watts symbolizes that there is redemption for sinners. And who is interested? Compare this symbolism with that in Michael Angelo's picture, where the just-created and half-awakened Adam raises his arm in superb languor to receive Divine knowledge by the touching of God's forefinger. I do not here include the picture "Love and Death," because it does not seem to me in any sense a religious picture. It suggests no dogma nor mystical theory, nor is there any kind of sentiment. The artist, by his labour, has placed before us in monumental effectiveness certain facts now and always with us. It is a great picture, but it is not a religious picture.

Watts is a portrait-painter beyond all praise; he is singular among all painters for the interest he imparts to his subject. Before most portraits people stand and say, "What dull things portraits are! why are they ever exhibited?" or perhaps they say, "What a clever painter! but what an ugly man to paint!" In presence of a Watts we are interested in a face; we feel liking or aversion, or a tantalizing curiosity.

In Watts' portraits craftsmanship attains its perfection, because here he worked in an atmosphere of exacting criticism; everyone understands a portrait, and the stupidest is interested when it is his own portrait.

When Watts painted his imaginative work, it was done in an atmosphere of polite indifference. It is a strange paradox that Watts lived surrounded by the most distinguished and intellectual society of his time, and yet he worked in solitude. When he went wrong, there was no one to tell him; and when he was right, equally there was no response. They were interested in the artist, but not in his art. This lofty-minded recluse, who laboured by his painting to give the world great thoughts, impressed these cultivated worldlings: they were interested in the man, but neither in his thoughts nor in his pictures. At a private view in the Grosvenor Gallery a friend of mine overheard Watts saying to a lady: "Everyone is interested in my velvet coat, but no one asks me about my pictures."

It was not so in ancient Italy. When Michael Angelo, at the imperious command of the impetuous Pope Julius, uncovered half his work on the ceiling of the Sistine Chapel, he stood to receive the judgment of a people who were superstitious, ignorant men of violence, men of war, homicidal, but each one of them impassioned for Art.

"Italy," said the Spanish painter to Michael Angelo, "produces the best Art, because Italians hate mediocrity." We are clay in the hands of the potter. We may affect to be proud and solitary as Lucifer, but in vain; the artist gives that he may receive; to seek sympathy and desire companionship is as instinctive as hunger and thirst. To the true artist exacting criticism is comforting as mother's love; and, wanting this exacting criticism, Watts fell away into slackness of work and of thought.

We can only say that had he lived in Dublin his fate would have been worse. Indifference, however polite and respectful, is bad; but destructive criticism kills.

There was once a small but mighty nation, now numerous as the sands of the seashore, and no longer so interesting. To this nation was born a poet, and they made him the poet of all time. They took him and taught him all they knew—and they had great things to teach; and when, at their command, he made great dramas, they stood at his elbow; and everything they gave him he gave back to them tenfold.

England was then Shakespeare's land.

The poet is always amongst us: the difficulty is

how to find him; he is like the proverbial needle in a bundle of hay.

But one thing is certain—logicians without love will not find him; they leave a desolation, and call it peace—nay, they call it culture. Critics of this sort will allow nothing to exist except themselves. No; I am wrong. There is one thing they admire more even than themselves—the *fait accompli*, a mundane success. Had Watts been born in Dublin, he would have read for the " Indian Civil," and perhaps—passed.

J. B. YEATS, R.H.A.

1907.